Cultural Traditions in
South Africa

Molly
Aloian

Crabtree Publishing Company
www.crabtreebooks.com

Crabtree Publishing Company

www.crabtreebooks.com

Author: Molly Aloian
Publishing plan research and development:
  Reagan Miller
Project coordinator: Kathy Middleton
Editor: Kelly Spence
Proofreaders: Marcia Abramson, Wendy Scavuzzo
Design: Tibor Choleva
Photo research: Melissa McClellan
Production coordinator and prepress technician:
  Tammy McGarr
Print coordinator: Margaret Amy Salter

Produced and Designed by BlueAppleWorks Inc.

Cover: Traditional South African costume (center); Protea, South African flowering plant (upper left); Elephant (lower left); Elands Fig (upper right); Blue Crane Bird (middle right); Wooden bongos (lower right); samosa (bottom middle)

Title page: African American Man with football on Table Mountain beach

Photographs:
Dreamstime: © Photographerlondon: page 1; © smole08: page 15 (insert); © Photka: page 30 (top insert)
Getty Images: Frank Trimbos/Gallo Images: page 12; Gallo Images (Pty) Ltd: page 27
Istock: page 29
Stella Duong: pages 9 (top), 28
Shutterstock: © T.W. van Urk cover (upper left); © Anna Omelchenko cover (center); © Neil Bradfield cover (middle right); © Danie Nel cover (upper right); © michaeljung cover (bottom centre); © mythja cover (bottom right); © David Steele cover (bottom left); © Galyna Andrushko cover (background); ©AridOcean: page 4 (left); © Rainer Lesniewski: page 4 (right); © Neil Bradfield: page 5; © Jaxons: pages 6, 7, 17; © michaeljung: pages 8, 16–17 (background), 22 (top); © Gordon Bell: pages 8–9 (background), 30–31 (background); © meunierd: pages 9 (bottom), 15 (bottom), 18 (left); © urbancowboy page 11 (inset); © InnaFelker page 11; © Nolte Lourens page 18 (inset), page 21 (bottom), 26 (right); © Luchi_a : page 19 (right); © MickyWiswedel page 20; © Wolf Avni: pages 21 (top), 22 (bottom), 30; © milosk50: page 23 (top); © James Jones Jr: page 23 (bottom); © PhotoSky: page 25 (inset); © Photo Africa: page 25 (top) © Rudi Venter: page 25 (bottom); © Four Oaks: page 26 (left); © Anna Hoychuk: page 31 (inset)
Thinkstock: MickyWiswedel: page 16
Wikimedia Commons: Albinfo: page 19 (left); russavia: page 24

Library and Archives Canada Cataloguing in Publication

Aloian, Molly, author
    Cultural traditions in South Africa / Molly Aloian.

(Cultural traditions in my world)
Includes index.
Issued in print and electronic formats.
ISBN 978-0-7787-0304-4 (bound).--ISBN 978-0-7787-0316-7 (pbk.).--
ISBN 978-1-4271-7488-8 (html).--ISBN 978-1-4271-7494-9 (pdf)

    1. Holidays--South Africa--Juvenile literature. 2. South Africa--Social life and customs--Juvenile literature. I. Title. II. Series: Cultural traditions in my world

GT4889.S7A56 2014   j394.26968   C2014-900911-9
                                           C2014-900912-7

Library of Congress Cataloging-in-Publication Data

CIP available at the Library of Congress

Crabtree Publishing Company
www.crabtreebooks.com   1-800-387-7650

Printed in the USA/052014/SN20140313

Published in Canada
Crabtree Publishing
616 Welland Ave.
St. Catharines, ON
L2M 5V6

Published in the United States
Crabtree Publishing
PMB 59051
350 Fifth Avenue, 59th Floor
New York, New York 10118

Published in the United Kingdom
Crabtree Publishing
Maritime House
Basin Road North, Hove
BN41 1WR

Published in Australia
Crabtree Publishing
3 Charles Street
Coburg North
VIC 3058

Contents

Welcome to South Africa

Over 52 million people live in South Africa, a country located at the southern end of Africa. South Africa is a vibrant country with 11 official languages that represent the different cultural groups living there. However, the people of South Africa have had a long and challenging history to become the **multicultural** nation it is today.

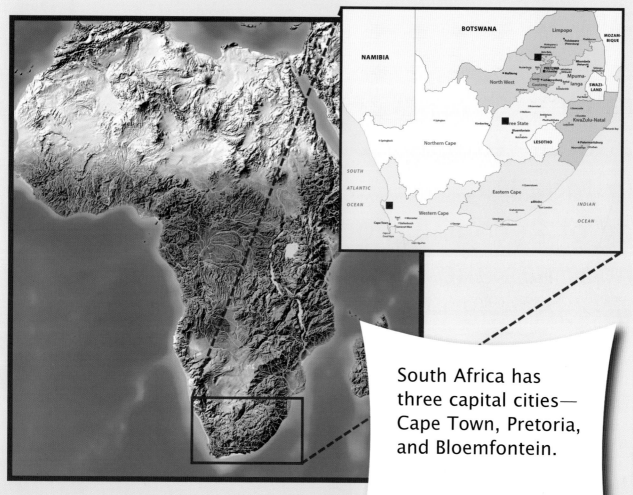

South Africa has three capital cities—Cape Town, Pretoria, and Bloemfontein.

Cultural traditions are holidays, festivals, special days, and customs that groups of people celebrate. Many holidays in South Africa remember an important day in the history of the country. Others are for religious celebrations or to recognize the contributions of an individual or group of people.

Did You Know?
Most South Africans can speak two or more languages. The official languages include: Afrikaans, English, Ndebele, Northern Sotho, Sotho, Swazi, Tswana, Tsonga, Venda, Xhosa and Zulu.

South Africa has many people from many cultures. It has not been easy, but they have learned to celebrate each other.

Living Separately

In the past, people in South Africa were separated according to **race**. This was called **apartheid**. Black people and mixed race people were forced to live separately from white people. Black people were not allowed to work, go to school, travel, or even play sports with white people. They did not have the same **human rights** and freedoms as white people. Apartheid ended in 1994. Today, Africans of all colors share the same opportunities as everyone else.

Buses, schools, and all other activities are shared by all people equally in present-day South Africa.

BLANKES WHITES

NIE — BLANKES NON — WHITES

Your ticket to the museum has randomly classified you as either 'white' or 'non-white'. Please use the entrance to the museum indicated on the front of your ticket.

RACE CLASSIFICATION

Racial classification was the foundation of all apartheid laws. It placed individuals in one of four groups: African, described as 'Bantu' in apartheid laws, 'coloured', 'Asian' or 'white'. To illustrate the everyday reality, visitors are arbitrarily classified as either white or non-white. You will only be permitted to enter through the gate allocated to your race group. Identity documents, like those which you see on both sides of the corridor, were the main tools used to implement this racial divide.

JOURNEYS

THE BIRTH OF THE STRUGGLE

JOHANNESBURG PANORAMA

Did You Know?
After apartheid ended in 1994, the new government decided to change all the national holidays to new ones that reflected South Africa's new identity as one nation with equal opportunities for all its people.

Apartheid is now part of history. People of all races can learn about it by visiting the Apartheid Museum in Johannesburg.

The Rainbow Nation

South Africa's rainbow of cultures include native African peoples and people who came to South Africa from other countries. White settlers, including Afrikaners and the British, brought many traditions to South Africa during **colonial** times. Today, people of all races celebrate many of the same traditions as one nation.

Did You Know?
South Africa has been nicknamed the "rainbow nation" because of its unique mix of different cultural groups.

Xhosa women sing and perform a traditional dance.

Many ethnic groups, such as the Zulu and Xhosa, continue to celebrate their ancestors' culture through music, rituals, dance, and other art forms. This vibrant mix of new and old cultures make South Africa one of the most multicultural countries in the world.

Did You Know?
The Zulu people make up the largest ethnic group in South Africa. The name "Zulu" means "people of heaven."

9

New Year's Day

Many South Africans celebrate the start of a new year on January 1. People have the day off from work and school. New Year's celebrations usually take place outdoors because January falls in the middle of summer in South Africa. Families and friends often gather together on the evening of December 31 and count down to midnight as the old year ends. A huge New Year's celebration takes place at the foot of Table Mountain, a famous mountain that overlooks the city of Cape Town. Over 80,000 people gather to enjoy the fireworks and street performances.

Did You Know?
In Cape Town, many people also celebrate the day after New Year's. This day is called *Tweede Nuwe Jaar*, or Second New Year. People celebrate with musical performances and dress up in costumes.

Table Mountain's name comes from its shape. The top of the mountain is flat like a table.

Human Rights Day

March 21 is an important holiday in South Africa. It is Human Rights Day. On this day in 1960, a terrible event occurred. Outside a police station in the town of Sharpeville police killed 69 black people and seriously wounded 180 other.
The people were holding a peaceful **protest** against apartheid laws they believed were unfair.

On Human Rights Day, relatives of the victims of the 1960 Sharpeville Massacre gather in cemeteries for memorial ceremonies.

All children can go to school together now in South Africa. This is one of the freedoms achieved by the human rights fighters of the past.

On Human Rights Day, South Africans remember and honor the people who were killed and wounded in Sharpeville. The day reminds South Africans of those who suffered and lost their lives in the fight to end apartheid.

Did You Know?
The names of the men, women, and children who were shot in Sharpeville are all written on a special memorial plaque outside of the police station in Sharpeville.

Easter and Family Day

Easter usually takes place in March or April. On Easter, Christians remember the death and **resurrection** of Jesus Christ. South Africans also celebrate Easter with a special meal. On Easter Sunday, a large Easter egg hunt takes place each year on Table Mountain in Cape Town.

Many South African families go hiking or canoeing during the long Easter weekend.

In South Africa, many people started taking an extra day off of work after Easter. The day was called Easter Monday, but was renamed Family Day in 1995. On Family Day, people have the day off work and school to spend quality time with family and friends. Family members and friends have barbecues, play games, or do crafts together. Some go away for a long weekend.

Did You Know?
In South Africa, it is traditional to eat pickled fish on Good Friday. Good Friday is a Christian holiday celebrated two days before Easter.

Kids play outside during their Easter vacation from school.

Hot cross buns are a popular food to eat on Easter Sunday.

Freedom Day

On April 27, South Africans celebrate Freedom Day. On this day in 1994, all South Africans, including black people and mixed race people, were allowed to vote for the first time. It was the first **democratic** election in South Africa.

People wait in line to vote in a South African election. Voting allows all citizens to have their voice heard in who represents them in their government.

There are all kinds of social events, including speeches and ceremonies, throughout the country on Freedom Day. People remember and honor those who fought to gain freedom for themselves and others.

In 1994, South Africans elected Nelson Mandela as president. He was the first black president of South Africa. He was president until 1999.

Youth Day

South Africans celebrate Youth Day each year on June 16. This day reminds people of tragic events in an area called Soweto in 1976. In Soweto, police killed hundreds of black schoolchildren who were holding a protest in the streets. The schoolchildren were protesting the use of Afrikaans and English in schools full of black students who wanted to speak their traditional languages.

South African kids now can study in their native language.

On Youth Day, people in Soweto lay flowers at the Hector Pieterson Memorial. Hector Pieterson was one of the first young boys to be shot in the Soweto protests in 1976.

On this day, South Africans remind themselves of how important young people are and how to protect them from other acts of violence. They also celebrate the end of the unfair apartheid government. They participate in marches, make banners, and shout out special cheers and songs.

Did You Know?
The Soweto Gospel Choir is a South African singing group that formed in 2002 and performs all over the world. They received a Grammy Award in 2007.

Workers' Day

On Workers' Day, South Africans take time to respect and honor the important role of the workforce in South Africa. In the past, South Africans had to work very hard for long hours and often did not receive fair pay. Many people also worked in unsafe conditions and felt they had no rights. People began asking for higher wages and safer working conditions. They asked for more rights within the workforce.

Did You Know?
South Africa is just one of about 80 countries around the world that celebrate the contributions of workers on May 1 each year.

South African workers have held many marches and rallies to demand fair working conditions.

This holiday has special importance in South Africa because of the contributions of the workforce while protesting apartheid.

Today, May 1 is a day to celebrate the many achievements of workers and their fight for better working conditions.

Grahamstown Art Festival

This annual festival is one of Africa's largest and most colorful arts and culture festivals since 1976. For ten days in July, people of all races come together to enjoy art, dance, and music. Visitors from all over the country and the world travel to Grahamstown to participate in this important cultural event.

These women are performing a traditional Zulu dance. At the Grahamstown festival, events take place in many languages, including Afrikaans, Zulu, and Xhosa.

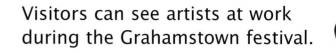
Visitors can see artists at work during the Grahamstown festival.

Many people attend the festival to see how art, dance, and music reflect the many social and cultural changes that have taken place in South Africa since the end of apartheid. There are special awards for creative music, drama, dance, jazz, and visual art.

National Women's Day

Each year, South Africans celebrate National Women's Day on August 9. People commemorate the thousands of women from all over the country who organized a huge march to protest the laws of the apartheid government in 1956.

South African women celebrate at one of many events held for National Women's Day.

South African women now can choose modern careers or traditional life.

On National Women's Day, South Africans celebrate the strength and determination of women. People give speeches and hold special ceremonies that highlight the important role of women in South Africa. Young girls talk to their mothers, sisters, aunts, and other women about how they can continue to contribute to South African society and culture.

Did You Know?
Over 20,000 women marched in protest to the Union Buildings in Pretoria on August 9, 1956.

Heritage Day

South Africans celebrate their unique **heritage** and culture on Heritage Day, which takes place on September 24 each year. South Africans believe that it is the country's many **diverse** cultural groups that help keep it growing and strong. They are proud of their country's diverse population and celebrate this on Heritage Day.

Students learn about their ancestry for Heritage Day. They take pride in their different cultures.

Did You Know?
The South African flag has six colors— green, black, yellow, red, white, and blue. It is the only flag in the world with this many colors.

A typical Heritage Day celebration includes getting together with family, friends, and neighbors and cooking meat on the grill. In Afrikaans, the word *braai* means grill or barbecue. The braai brings people together to enjoy grilled fish or meat. Some people even eat grilled antelope or ostrich.

On Heritage Day, many South Africans like to be outdoors to braai the day away.

Day of Reconciliation

For several years, December 16 has been an important day in South Africa. On this day, people think about reconciliation, which means restoring friendly relationships and forgiving one another.

This rally celebrates the life of Nelson Mandela, South Africa's national hero.

Did You Know?
Nelson Mandela was more than just a president. He led South Africa away from apartheid and fought for people of all races to be treated equality and fairly.

Nelson Mandela died on December 6, 2013. People in South Africa and around the world celebrate Mandela Day on July 18 each year. This day is Nelson Mandela's birthday.

People try hard to forgive each other for past wrongdoings and events during the apartheid era. On Reconciliation Day in 2013, a bronze statue of Nelson Mandela was unveiled at the Union Buildings. This is where Nelson Mandela was **inaugurated** as South Africa's first elected president after apartheid.

Christmas and the Day of Goodwill

Christmas is a festive holiday in South Africa. In the days leading up to Christmas, people hang wreaths and stockings, decorate Christmas trees, and buy gifts for family members. Many children look forward to a visit from *Sinterklaas*, which means Santa Claus in Afrikaans. On Christmas Day, many Christians celebrate the birth of Jesus Christ by going to church services.

In South Africa, Christmas falls during the warm summer season. Christmas is also at the end of the school year, so children are off school following the holiday.

Many South African families enjoy a traditional Christmas dinner of roast beef, turkey, vegetables, mince pies, and plum pudding. Because it's summer, some have an open-air Christmas lunch instead of eating indoors. In the afternoon, families have fun together at parks and beaches.

The day after Christmas is called the Day of Goodwill. This is a day to remember the less fortunate, and to spend time with family and friends.

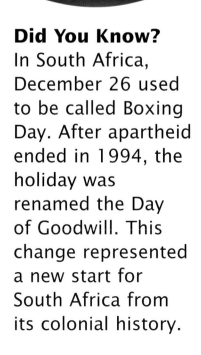

Did You Know?
In South Africa, December 26 used to be called Boxing Day. After apartheid ended in 1994, the holiday was renamed the Day of Goodwill. This change represented a new start for South Africa from its colonial history.

Glossary

ancestors People from whom others are descended

apartheid A system of government in South Africa that separated people based on their race

colonial Describing countries that were owned and ruled by the British monarch

democratic Describing a system of government in which every person has the power to vote and make decisions

diverse Having or showing great variety

heritage Things acquired from the past that have been passed down from previous generations

human rights Basic rights that every person should have

inaugurated Introduced into office with special ceremonies

multicultural Made up of several cultural or ethnic groups

protest To object or not approve of something, or to display disapproval

race A group of people that share the same culture, history, language, and physical characteristics

resurrection Coming back to life after death

Index